Spot the Difference
Picture Puzzles

Published 2021 by Parragon Books, Ltd.

Copyright © 2021 Cottage Door Press, LLC
5005 Newport Drive, Rolling Meadows, Illinois 60008

Puzzles created by diacriTech
Images used under license from Shutterstock.com

ISBN: 978-1-64638-024-4

Spot the Difference
Picture Puzzles

How to Play:

Spot the differences between the two nearly identical images. The number of differences is indicated at the top of each puzzle pair.

Having trouble? Try visually breaking the image into a grid and searching one quadrant at a time. Still can't find something? Take a peek at the solutions at the back of the book. *Happy hunting!*

41

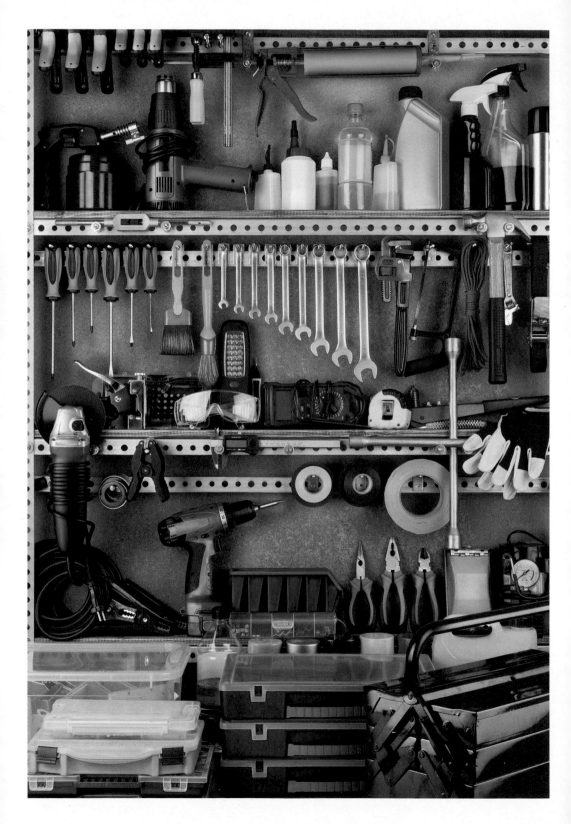

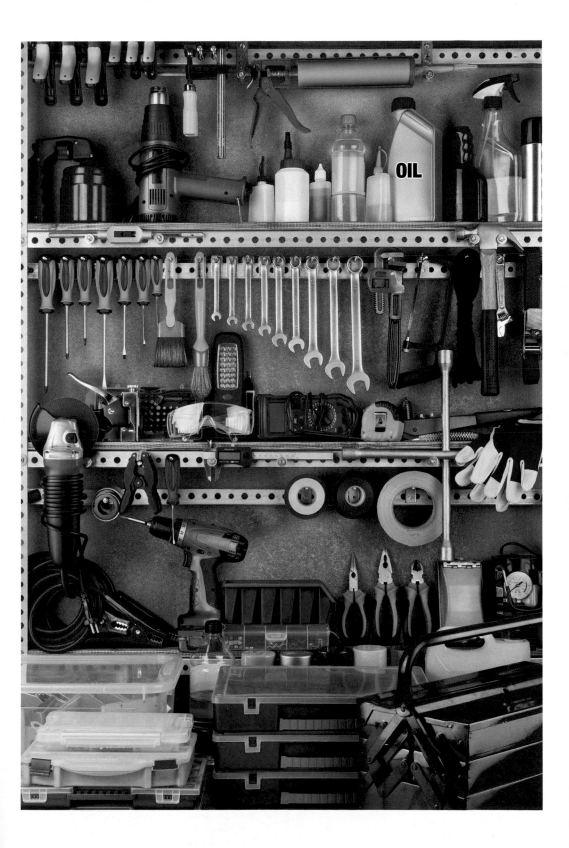

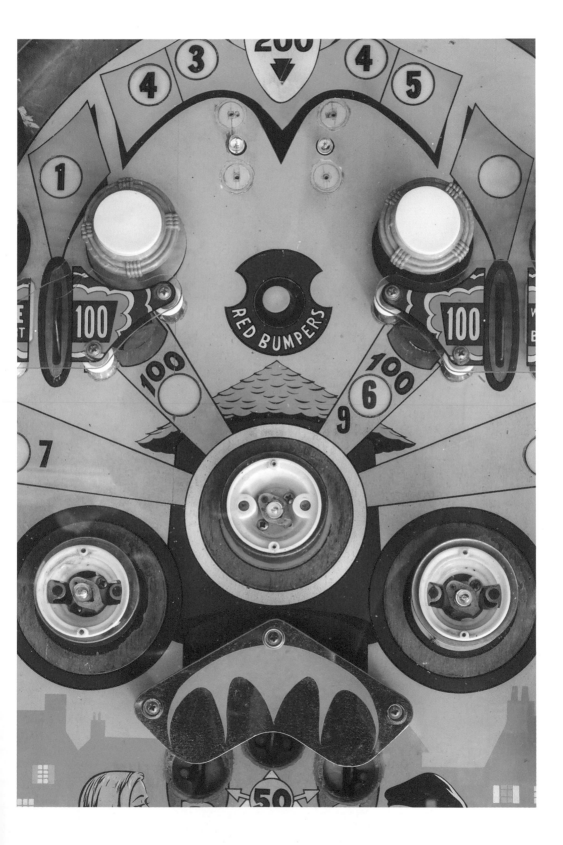

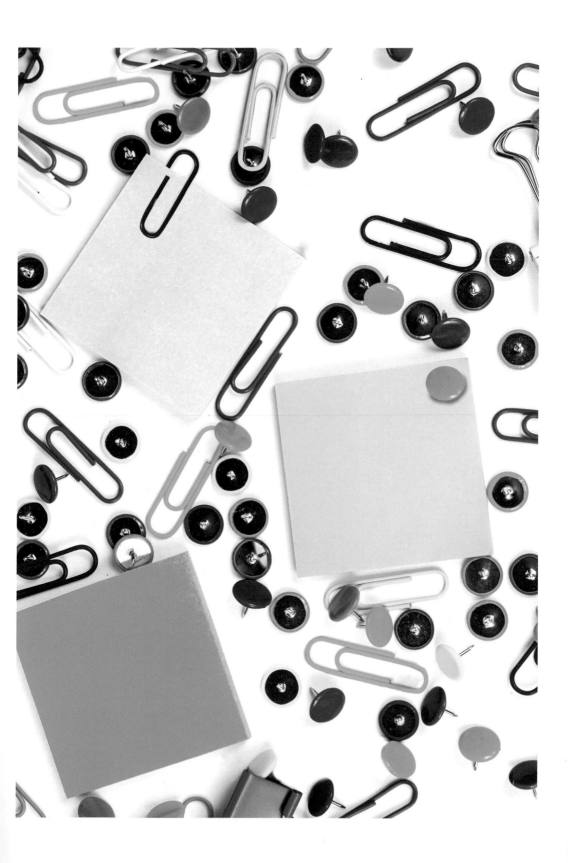

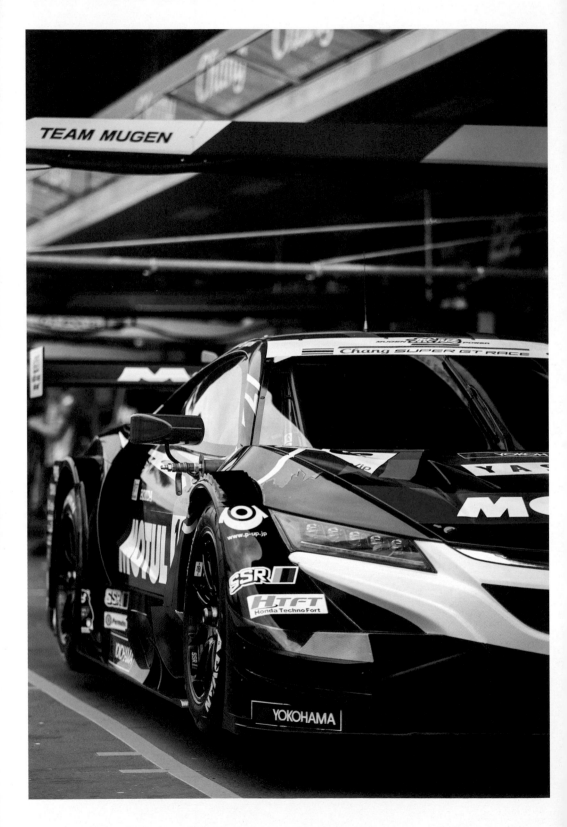

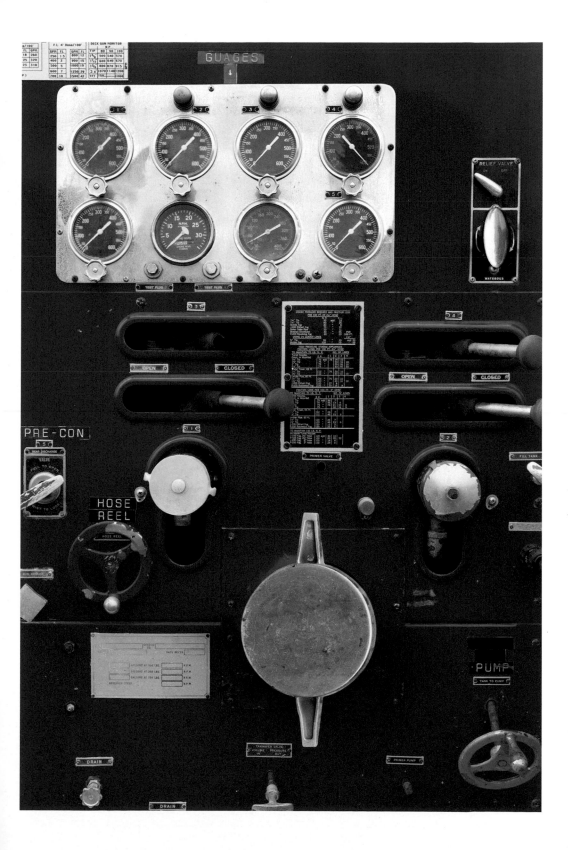

137

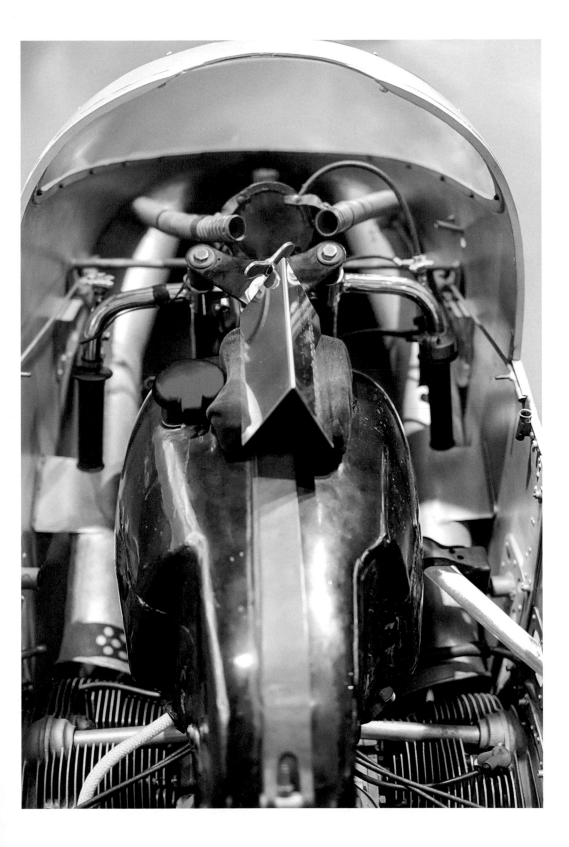

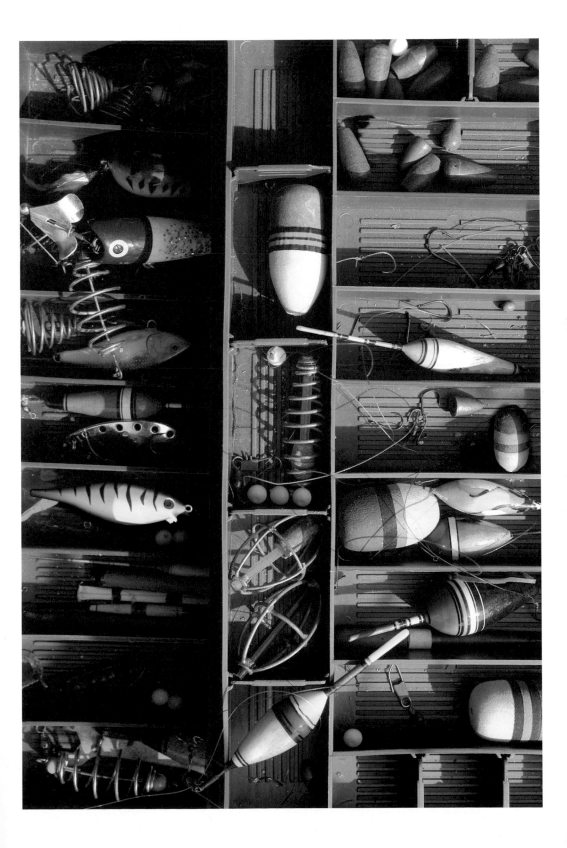

Solutions

Puzzle No. 1

Puzzle No. 2

Puzzle No. 3

Solutions

Puzzle No. 4

Puzzle No. 5

Puzzle No. 6

Solutions

Puzzle No. 7

Puzzle No. 8

Puzzle No. 9

Solutions

Puzzle No. 10

Puzzle No. 11

Puzzle No. 12

Solutions

Puzzle No. 13

Puzzle No. 14

Puzzle No. 15

Solutions

Puzzle No. 16

Puzzle No. 17

Puzzle No. 18

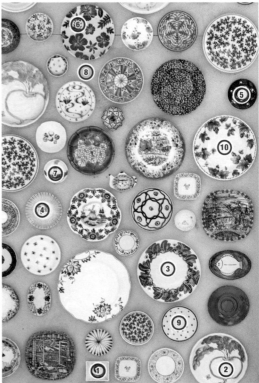

Solutions

Puzzle No. 19

Puzzle No. 20

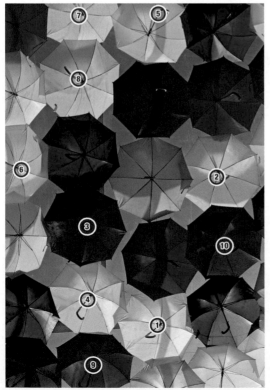

Puzzle No. 21

Solutions

Puzzle No. 22

Puzzle No. 23

Puzzle No. 24

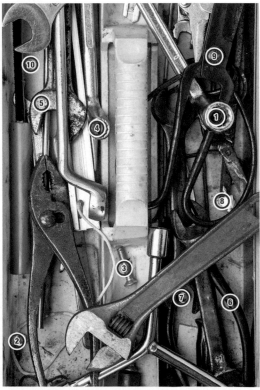

Solutions

Puzzle No. 25

Puzzle No. 26

Puzzle No. 27

Solutions

Puzzle No. 28

Puzzle No. 29

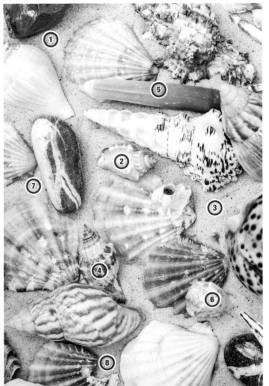

Puzzle No. 30

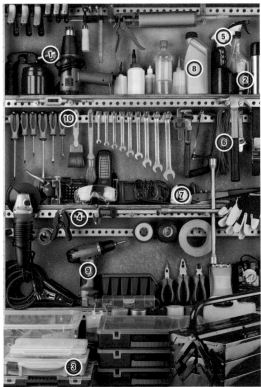

Solutions

Puzzle No. 31

Puzzle No. 32

Puzzle No. 33

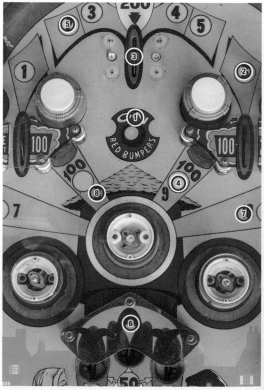

Solutions

Puzzle No. 34

Puzzle No. 35

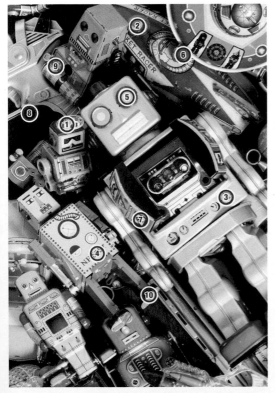

Puzzle No. 36

Solutions

Puzzle No. 37

Puzzle No. 38

Puzzle No. 39

Solutions

Puzzle No. 40

Puzzle No. 41

Puzzle No. 42

Solutions

Puzzle No. 43

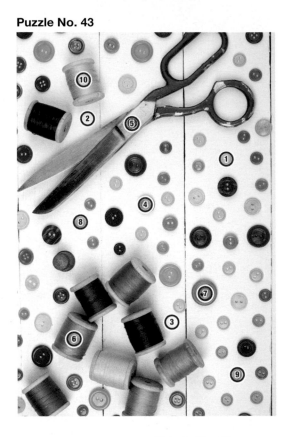

Puzzle No. 44

Puzzle No. 45

Solutions

Puzzle No. 46

Puzzle No. 47

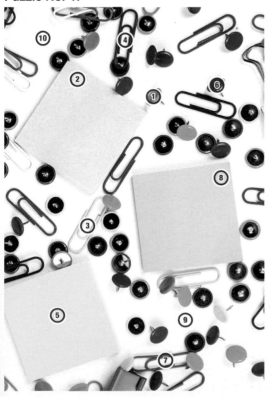

Puzzle No. 48

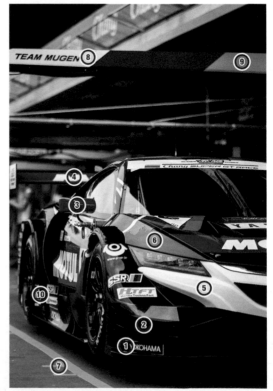

Solutions

Puzzle No. 49

Puzzle No. 50

Puzzle No. 51

Solutions

Puzzle No. 52

Puzzle No. 53

Puzzle No. 54

Solutions

Puzzle No. 55

Puzzle No. 56

Puzzle No. 57

Solutions

Puzzle No. 58

Puzzle No. 59

Puzzle No. 60

Solutions

Puzzle No. 61

Puzzle No. 62

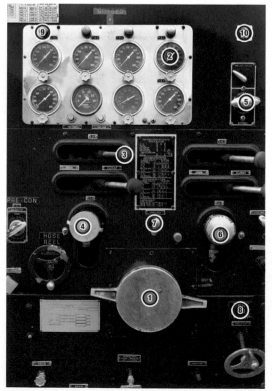

Puzzle No. 63

Solutions

Puzzle No. 64

Puzzle No. 65

Puzzle No. 66

Solutions

Puzzle No. 67

Puzzle No. 68

Puzzle No. 69

Solutions

Puzzle No. 70

Puzzle No. 71

Puzzle No. 72

Solutions

Puzzle No. 73

Puzzle No. 74

Puzzle No. 75

Solutions

Puzzle No. 76

Puzzle No. 77

Puzzle No. 78

Solutions

Puzzle No. 79

Puzzle No. 80

Solutions

Puzzle No. 81

Puzzle No. 82

Solutions

Puzzle No. 83

Puzzle No. 84

Solutions

Puzzle No. 85

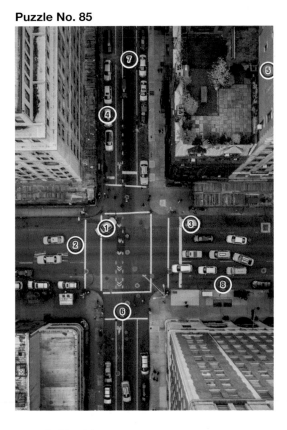

Puzzle No. 86

Solutions

Puzzle No. 87

Puzzle No. 88

Solutions

Puzzle No. 89

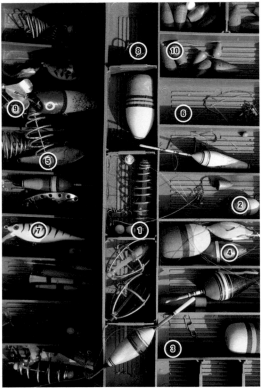

Puzzle No. 90

Solutions

Puzzle No. 91

Puzzle No. 92

Solutions

Puzzle No. 93

Puzzle No. 94

Solutions

Puzzle No. 95

Puzzle No. 96

Solutions

Puzzle No. 97

Puzzle No. 98

Solutions

Puzzle No. 99

Puzzle No. 100